The

GREAT IMPERSONATOR!

‑⊙℮ THE LOCHLAINN SEABROOK COLLECTION ℮⊙‑

AMERICAN CIVIL WAR
Abraham Lincoln Was a Liberal, Jefferson Davis Was a Conservative: The Missing Key to Understanding the American Civil War
Confederacy 101: Amazing Facts You Never Knew About America's Oldest Political Tradition
Confederate Blood and Treasure: An Interview With Lochlainn Seabrook
Everything You Were Taught About African-Americans and the Civil War is Wrong, Ask a Southerner!
Everything You Were Taught About the Civil War is Wrong, Ask a Southerner!
Give This Book to a Yankee! A Southern Guide to the Civil War For Northerners
Heroes of the Southern Confederacy: The Illustrated Book of Confederate Officials, Soldiers, and Civilians
Lincoln's War: The Real Cause, the Real Winner, the Real Loser
The Great Yankee Coverup: What the North Doesn't Want You to Know About Lincoln's War!
The Ultimate Civil War Quiz Book: How Much Do You Really Know About America's Most Misunderstood Conflict?
Women in Gray: A Tribute to the Ladies Who Supported the Southern Confederacy

CONFEDERATE MONUMENTS
Confederate Monuments: Why Every American Should Honor Confederate Soldiers and Their Memorials

CONFEDERATE FLAG
Confederate Flag Facts: What Every American Should Know About Dixie's Southern Cross
What the Confederate Flag Means to Me: Americans Speak Out in Defense of Southern Honor, Heritage, and History

SECESSION
All We Ask Is To Be Let Alone: The Southern Secession Fact Book

SLAVERY
Everything You Were Taught About American Slavery is Wrong, Ask a Southerner!
Slavery 101: Amazing Facts You Never Knew About America's "Peculiar Institution"
The Bittersweet Bond: Race Relations in the Old South as Described by White and Black Southerners

CHILDREN
Honest Jeff and Dishonest Abe: A Southern Children's Guide to the Civil War
Saddle, Sword, and Gun: A Biography of Nathan Bedford Forrest For Teens

NATHAN BEDFORD FORREST
A Rebel Born: A Defense of Nathan Bedford Forrest - Confederate General, American Legend (winner of the 2011 Jefferson Davis Historical Gold Medal)
A Rebel Born: The Screenplay (film about N. B. Forrest)
Forrest! 99 Reasons to Love Nathan Bedford Forrest
Give 'Em Hell Boys! The Complete Military Correspondence of Nathan Bedford Forrest
I Rode With Forrest! Confederate Soldiers Who Served With the World's Greatest Cavalry Leader
Nathan Bedford Forrest and African-Americans: Yankee Myth, Confederate Fact
Nathan Bedford Forrest and the Battle of Fort Pillow: Yankee Myth, Confederate Fact
Nathan Bedford Forrest and the Ku Klux Klan: Yankee Myth, Confederate Fact
Nathan Bedford Forrest: Southern Hero, American Patriot - Honoring a Confederate Icon and the Old South
Saddle, Sword, and Gun: A Biography of Nathan Bedford Forrest For Teens
The God of War: Nathan Bedford Forrest As He Was Seen By His Contemporaries
The Quotable Nathan Bedford Forrest: Selections From the Writings and Speeches of the Confederacy's Most Brilliant Cavalryman

QUOTABLE SERIES
The Alexander H. Stephens Reader: Excerpts From the Works of a Confederate Founding Father
The Quotable Alexander H. Stephens: Selections From the Writings and Speeches of the Confederacy's First Vice President
The Quotable Jefferson Davis: Selections From the Writings and Speeches of the Confederacy's First President
The Quotable Nathan Bedford Forrest: Selections From the Writings and Speeches of the Confederacy's Most Brilliant Cavalryman
The Quotable Robert E. Lee: Selections From the Writings and Speeches of the South's Most Beloved Civil War General
The Quotable Stonewall Jackson: Selections From the Writings and Speeches of the South's Most Famous General
The Unquotable Abraham Lincoln: The President's Quotes They Don't Want You To Know!

CIVIL WAR BATTLES
Encyclopedia of the Battle of Franklin - A Comprehensive Guide to the Conflict that Changed the Civil War
Nathan Bedford Forrest and the Battle of Fort Pillow: Yankee Myth, Confederate Fact
The Battle of Franklin: Recollections of Confederate and Union Soldiers
The Battle of Nashville: Recollections of Confederate and Union Soldiers
The Battle of Spring Hill: Recollections of Confederate and Union Soldiers

CONSTITUTIONAL HISTORY
America's Three Constitutions: Complete Texts of the Articles of Confederation, Constitution of the United States of America, and Constitution of the Confederate States of America
The Articles of Confederation Explained: A Clause-by-Clause Study of America's First Constitution
The Constitution of the Confederate States of America Explained: A Clause-by-Clause Study of the South's Magna Carta

VICTORIAN CONFEDERATE LITERATURE
I, Confederate: Why the South Seceded and Fought in the Words of 19th-Century Southerners
Rise Up and Call Them Blessed: Victorian Tributes to the Confederate Soldier, 1861-1901
Support Your Local Confederate: Wit and Humor in the Southern Confederacy
The Bittersweet Bond: Race Relations in the Old South as Described by White and Black Southerners
The God of War: Nathan Bedford Forrest As He Was Seen By His Contemporaries
The Old Rebel: Robert E. Lee As He Was Seen By His Contemporaries
Victorian Confederate Poetry: The Southern Cause in Verse, 1861-1901

ABRAHAM LINCOLN
Abraham Lincoln: The Southern View - Demythologizing America's Sixteenth President
Lincolnology: The Real Abraham Lincoln Revealed in His Own Words - A Study of Lincoln's Suppressed, Misinterpreted, and Forgotten Writings and Speeches
Lincoln's War: The Real Cause, the Real Winner, the Real Loser
The Great Impersonator! 99 Reasons to Dislike Abraham Lincoln
The Unholy Crusade: Lincoln's Legacy of Destruction in the American South
The Unquotable Abraham Lincoln: The President's Quotes They Don't Want You To Know!

NATURAL HISTORY
North America's Amazing Mammals: An Encyclopedia for the Whole Family
The Concise Book of Owls: A Guide to Nature's Most Mysterious Birds
The Concise Book of Tigers: A Guide to Nature's Most Remarkable Cats

PARANORMAL
Carnton Plantation Ghost Stories: True Tales of the Unexplained from Tennessee's Most Haunted Civil War House!
UFOs and Aliens: The Complete Guidebook

FAMILY HISTORIES
The Blakeneys: An Etymological, Ethnological, and Genealogical Study - Uncovering the Mysterious Origins of the Blakeney Family and Name
The Caudills: An Etymological, Ethnological, and Genealogical Study - Exploring the Name and National Origins of a European-American Family
The McGavocks of Carnton Plantation: A Southern History - Celebrating One of Dixie's Most Noble Confederate Families and Their Tennessee Home

MIND, BODY, SPIRIT
Autobiography of a Non-Yogi: A Scientist's Journey From Hinduism to Christianity (Dr. Amitava Dasgupta, with Lochlainn Seabrook)
Britannia Rules: Goddess-Worship in Ancient Anglo-Celtic Society - An Academic Look at the United Kingdom's Matricentric Spiritual Past
Christ Is All and In All: Rediscovering Your Divine Nature and the Kingdom Within
Christmas Before Christianity: How the Birthday of the "Sun" Became the Birthday of the "Son"
Jesus and the Gospel of Q: Christ's Pre-Christian Teachings As Recorded in the New Testament
Jesus and the Law of Attraction: The Bible-Based Guide to Creating Perfect Health, Wealth, and Happiness Following Christ's Simple Formula
Seabrook's Bible Dictionary of Traditional and Mystical Christian Doctrines
Sea Raven Press Blank Page Journal: For Reflections, Notes, and Sketches
The Bible and the Law of Attraction: 99 Teachings of Jesus, the Apostles, and the Prophets
The Book of Kelle: An Introduction to Goddess-Worship and the Great Celtic Mother-Goddess Kelle, Original Blessed Lady of Ireland
The Goddess Dictionary of Words and Phrases: Introducing a New Core Vocabulary for the Women's Spirituality Movement
The Martian Anomalies: A Photographic Search for Intelligent Life on Mars
Victorian Hernia Cures: Nonsurgical Self-Treatment of Inguinal Hernia
Vintage Southern Cookbook: 2,000 Delicious Dishes From Dixie

WOMEN
Aphrodite's Trade: The Hidden History of Prostitution Unveiled
Princess Diana: Modern Day Moon-Goddess - A Psychoanalytical and Mythological Look at Diana Spencer's Life, Marriage, and Death (with Dr. Jane Goldberg)
Women in Gray: A Tribute to the Ladies Who Supported the Southern Confederacy

REPRINTS
A Short History of the Confederate States of America (author Jefferson Davis; editor Lochlainn Seabrook)
Prison Life of Jefferson Davis (author John J. Craven; editor Lochlainn Seabrook)
Life of Beethoven (author Ludwig Nohl; editor Lochlainn Seabrook)
The New Revelation (author Arthur Conan Doyle; editor Lochlainn Seabrook)

Lochlainn Seabrook does not author books for fame and fortune, but for the love of writing and sharing his knowledge.

SeaRavenPress.com

Warning: *SEA RAVEN PRESS BOOKS WILL EXPAND YOUR ★MIND!*

The GREAT IMPERSONATOR!

99 Reasons To Dislike Abraham Lincoln

BY "THE VOICE OF THE TRADITIONAL SOUTH," COLONEL

LOCHLAINN SEABROOK

JEFFERSON DAVIS HISTORICAL GOLD MEDAL WINNER

Diligently Researched for the Elucidation of the Reader

2012

SEA RAVEN PRESS, NASHVILLE, TENNESSEE, USA

THE GREAT IMPERSONATOR!

Published by
Sea Raven Press, Cassidy Ravensdale, President
Nashville, Tennessee, USA
SeaRavenPress.com

SEA RAVEN PRESS
SOUTHERN BOOKS, REAL HISTORY!

PRINTING HISTORY
1st SRP paperback edition, 1st printing, October 2012; 2nd printing, June 2018; 3rd printing, September 2022 • ISBN: 978-0-9858632-2-7
1st SRP hardcover edition, 1st printing, June 2018; 2nd printing, September 2022 • ISBN: 978-1-943737-68-0

ISBN: 978-0-9858632-2-7 (paperback)
Library of Congress Control Number: 2012950368

The Great Impersonator! 99 Reasons To Dislike Abraham Lincoln, by Lochlainn
Seabrook. Includes endnotes and bibliographical references.

Front and back cover design and art, book design, layout, and interior art by Lochlainn Seabrook
All images, graphic design, graphic art, and illustrations copyright © Lochlainn Seabrook
All images selected, placed, manipulated, and/or created by Lochlainn Seabrook
Cover photo: The Lincoln Memorial, Washington, D.C., redesigned by Lochlainn Seabrook

The views documented in this book concerning the War for Southern Independence are those of the publisher.

WRITTEN, DESIGNED, PUBLISHED   IN THE UNITED STATES OF AMERICA

SEA RAVEN PRESS

Dedication

To my Conservative Southern ancestors.
They saw Abraham Lincoln for who he really was.

Epigraph

"Amid the universal din of praise that it has become the fashion to sing of Lincoln, only the student remembers the real facts, only the student knows not only that the Lincoln of the popular imagination of today bears little or no resemblance to the real Lincoln, but that the deification of Lincoln was planned and carried out by the members of his own party, by men who but a few short hours before Booth's bullet did its deadly work at Ford's theater, were reviling him as a buffoon, a coarse, vulgar jester. History affords no stranger spectacle than this, that today, nearly forty years after his death, the American people, North and South, have come to regard almost as a god a man who, when living, and up to the very hour of his death, was looked upon with contempt by nearly every man of his own party who intimately knew him, even by members of his Cabinet, by Senators, Congressmen, preachers and plain citizens."

Elizabeth Avery Meriwether

1904

CONTENTS

Notes to the Reader - page 11
Introduction, by Lochlainn Seabrook - page 12

Reason 1 - page 15
Reason 2 - page 16
Reason 3 - page 17
Reason 4 - page 18
Reason 5 - page 19
Reason 6 - page 20
Reason 7 - page 21
Reason 8 - page 22
Reason 9 - page 23
Reason 10 - page 24
Reason 11 - page 25
Reason 12 - page 26
Reason 13 - page 27
Reason 14 - page 28
Reason 15 - page 29
Reason 16 - page 30
Reason 17 - page 31
Reason 18 - page 32
Reason 19 - page 33
Reason 20 - page 34
Reason 21 - page 35
Reason 22 - page 36

Reason 23 - page 37
Reason 24 - page 38
Reason 25 - page 39
Reason 26 - page 40
Reason 27 - page 41
Reason 28 - page 42
Reason 29 - page 43
Reason 30 - page 44
Reason 31 - page 45
Reason 32 - page 46
Reason 33 - page 47
Reason 34 - page 48
Reason 35 - page 49
Reason 36 - page 50
Reason 37 - page 51
Reason 38 - page 52
Reason 39 - page 53
Reason 40 - page 54
Reason 41 - page 55
Reason 42 - page 56
Reason 43 - page 57
Reason 44 - page 58

Reason 45 - page 59
Reason 46 - page 60
Reason 47 - page 61
Reason 48 - page 62
Reason 49 - page 63
Reason 50 - page 64
Reason 51 - page 65
Reason 52 - page 66
Reason 53 - page 67
Reason 54 - page 68
Reason 55 - page 69
Reason 56 - page 70
Reason 57 - page 71
Reason 58 - page 72
Reason 59 - page 73
Reason 60 - page 74
Reason 61 - page 75
Reason 62 - page 76
Reason 63 - page 77
Reason 64 - page 78
Reason 65 - page 79
Reason 66 - page 80
Reason 67 - page 81
Reason 68 - page 82
Reason 69 - page 83
Reason 70 - page 84
Reason 71 - page 85
Reason 72 - page 86

Reason 73 - page 87
Reason 74 - page 88
Reason 75 - page 89
Reason 76 - page 90
Reason 77 - page 91
Reason 78 - page 92
Reason 79 - page 93
Reason 80 - page 94
Reason 81 - page 95
Reason 82 - page 96
Reason 83 - page 97
Reason 84 - page 98
Reason 85 - page 99
Reason 86 - page 100
Reason 87 - page 101
Reason 88 - page 102
Reason 89 - page 103
Reason 90 - page 104
Reason 91 - page 105
Reason 92 - page 106
Reason 93 - page 107
Reason 94 - page 108
Reason 95 - page 109
Reason 96 - page 110
Reason 97 - page 111
Reason 98 - page 112
Reason 99 - page 113

Notes - page 114
Bibliography - page 118
Meet the Author - page 120
Learn More - 121

NOTES TO THE READER

THE TWO MAIN POLITICAL PARTIES IN 1860

☛ In any study of the "Civil War" it is vitally important to keep in mind that the two major political parties were then the opposite of what they are today. The Democrats of the mid 19th Century were conservatives, akin to the Republican Party of today, while the Republicans of the mid 19th Century were liberals, akin to the Democratic Party of today. Thus the Confederacy's Democratic president, Jefferson Davis, was a conservative (with libertarian leanings); the Union's Republican president, Abraham Lincoln, was a liberal (with socialistic leanings).

Without a basic understanding of these facts, the American "Civil War" will forever remain incomprehensible. For a full discussion of this topic see my book, *Abraham Lincoln Was a Liberal, Jefferson Davis Was a Conservative: The Missing Key to Understanding the American Civil War*.

PRESENTISM

☛ As a historian I view *presentism* (judging the past according to present day mores and customs) as the enemy of authentic history. And this is precisely why the Left employs it in its ongoing war against traditional American, conservative, and Christian values. By looking at history through the lens of modern day beliefs—and, just as heinous, fabricating obviously fake history based on emotion, opinion, and political ideology—they are able to distort, revise, and reshape the past into a false narrative that fits their ideological agenda: the liberalization *and* Northernization of America, the enlargement and

Judging our ancestors by our own standards is unfair, unjust, misleading, and unethical.

further centralization of the national government, and total control of American political, economic, and social power, the same agenda that Lincoln championed.[1]

This book rejects presentism and replaces it with what I call *historicalism*: judging our ancestors based on the values of their own time. To get the most from this work the reader is invited to reject presentism as well. In this way—along with casting aside preconceived notions and the bogus "history" churned out by our left-wing education system—the truth in this work will be most readily ascertained and absorbed; truth that has been rigorously researched and forensically uncovered by myself using the scientific method. As Confederate Colonel Bennett H. Young noted in 1901:

> History is valuable only as it is true. Opinions concerning acts are not history; acts themselves alone are historic.[2]

LEARN MORE

☛ Lincoln's War on the American people and the Constitution can never be fully understood without a thorough knowledge of the South's perspective. As this book is only meant to be a brief introductory guide to these topics, one cannot hope to learn the complete story here. For those who are interested in additional material from Dixie's viewpoint, please see my comprehensive histories listed on pages 2 and 3.

INTRODUCTION

his is my fourth book (of five) on U.S. President Abraham Lincoln, who far from being the Great Emancipator (as the uneducated like to refer to him), should actually be called the Great Impersonator, my name for the dishonest, hypocritical, and fraudulent charlatan—who, though dead for 150 years, is still duping the masses to this day.

All five of my Lincoln books, when added up, total years of intensive labor and over 2,000 footnoted pages of heavily researched text. While I am generally happiest working on a book, it is never a pleasurable experience spending time with a historical figure you have no love for. As such, many have asked me how I am able to write about someone like Lincoln, someone who, here in Dixie, we rightly equate with radical Leftists, socialists, communists, racists, and dictators—as readers of this book will soon learn for themselves.

The simple answer is that as a Southern author and historian it is my responsibility to tell the truth and to disseminate it to as many people as possible. The sure knowledge that through my books thousands will learn the real facts about Lincoln and his war is both highly motivational and gratifying.

Though I subtitled this work "99 Reasons to Dislike Abraham Lincoln" this was only due to space constraints. Actually, here in the American South we have at least 2 million reasons to loathe our sixteenth chief executive, for this is how many of our people (of all races) died during the War between 1861 and 1865. We estimate that 1 million Northerners perished as well, all 3 million deaths directly stemming from the greed, aggressiveness, and insanity of the man who was intentionally and sarcastically nicknamed "Honest Abe" due to his lifelong propensity for double dealing, duplicity, and treachery.

Here, both Lincoln and his war, long incorrectly known by the North's self-serving and purposefully misleading term the American "Civil War," will be exposed for what they really were: Lincoln, a crafty and unscrupulous, demagogic, big government Liberal, wanted to overturn the Constitution, consolidate Left-wing political power in Washington, D.C., and impose his socialistic, racist dream on a Conservative, racially tolerant Southern populace. When Dixie resisted Northernization, Lincoln placed sympathetic Yankee states under

Steeped in over a century and a half of lies, myths, and gaslighting, Lincoln's cult has become ubiquitous.

martial law, threatened war on any European nation that interfered, and invaded the legally formed Southern Confederacy, all in an effort to crush states' rights and the will of the American people. Thank God Lincoln failed in both attempts.

Am I being too hard on the man that even his own party members referred to as a "baboon," a "vulgar clown," the "original gorilla," and "that damned idiot in the White House"? Read on and decide for yourself.

Colonel Lochlainn Seabrook, SCV
Franklin, Williamson County, Tennessee
October 2012

The
GREAT
IMPERSONATOR!

99 Reasons To Dislike
ABRAHAM LINCOLN

SEA RAVEN PRESS
NASHVILLE ❧ TENNESSEE
EST. 1995

"Books invite all; they constrain none."
Hartley Burr Alexander (1873-1939)

Reason 1

As a young attorney Lincoln defended not slaves, but slave owners. During this same period he was known to make public pronouncements in local Illinois newspapers showing his support for white supremacy.[3]

Reason 2

Lincoln lied about his military background, claiming he was a "military hero" in the Black Hawk War. "I fought, bled, and came away," he fibbed to the U.S. House of Representatives on July 27, 1848. In reality, he actually never saw a single day of combat or even a single Indian during the conflict.[4]

Reason 3

Lincoln, the man that uninformed Lincolnites continue to deify and often even liken to Jesus, was actually a lifelong atheist and an ardent anti-Christian. A true skeptic, a humanist, and—as his friends and family knew him—a proud self-proclaimed "infidel," Lincoln openly opposed organized religion, regularly told blasphemous stories, denounced his wife's spirituality, never prayed, never attended church, never joined any religious faith or denomination, never opened a Bible, never mentioned Jesus, and was well-known for his lack of belief in the divinity of Christ, Christian salvation, the sanctity of the Bible, and God himself. Lincoln even once wrote a "little book" declaring Jesus a "bastard" while asserting that the Bible's miracles went against the laws of Nature.[5] It is ironic indeed that the motto "In God We Trust" appeared for the first time on a Lincoln cent.[6]

Reason 4

Lincoln won the 1860 presidential election with only 39.8 percent of the ballots cast. Indeed, a mere one out of every seventeen eligible whites voted for him that November out of the total U.S. population.[7] How did he win then? The answer is the Electoral College (note that all of his electoral votes came from non-Southern states). But he would have lost even the electoral vote had he and his cronies not heavily engaged themselves in well publicized bribery, lying, horse-trading, patronage, and cheating.[8]

Reason 5

In early 1861, as the saber rattling and threats against the South from warmonger Lincoln escalated, Confederate President Jefferson Davis sent a peace commission to Washington in an attempt to avoid bloodshed between the two regions. "All we ask is to be let alone," he repeatedly told Lincoln.[9] Davis kept up this practice even after the War began. Lincoln, of course, ignored the South's pleas for peace, and, in fact, refused to have an official meeting with Confederate diplomats until February 3, 1865, by which time he already knew that the North would win the conflict. Even then he would not budge on his terms ("unconditional surrender"), and refused to recognize the Confederate ambassadors as envoys of a legitimate foreign country.[10]

Reason 6

As the correspondence between Lincoln and his cabinet solemnly testify, on April 12, 1861, the Yankee president intentionally tricked the Confederacy into firing the first shot at Fort Sumter, opening the conflict that he so desperately needed in order to implement big government in Washington.[11]

Reason 7

On April 15, 1861, Lincoln declared war on the South, an illegal act since the Constitution gives the president no such power. As Article 1, Section 8, Clause 11 of the Constitution clearly stipulates, only Congress possesses the authority to do so.[12] He also spent $2 million ($52 million in today's currency) to launch his war, also without congressional approval.[13] The consequences and fallout from Lincoln's War have lasted into the present day, leaving an emotional wound between the South and the North that will never completely heal.

Reason 8

As Lincoln's war on the South and the Constitution started to spread across North America, he began committing (and sanctioning) a long litany of infamous crimes. As the War progressed these came to include untold numbers of violations of the Geneva Conventions and crimes against both the Constitution and humanity.[14] For example, Lincoln sanctioned war crimes under the commands of countless U.S. officers, among them Yankee Generals Ulysses S. Grant, Philip H. Sheridan, and William T. Sherman. As a "reward" to such war criminals, Lincoln dined with them, personally thanked them, promoted them, and helped push through the "Thanks of Congress" award, which he had handed out like candy to such Union officers for achieving "significant victories."[15]

Reason 9

Though not an actual socialist or
communist, big government Liberal
Lincoln had radically progressive
tendencies nonetheless—as this very
book proves. For instance, he once
invited representatives of a socialist
organization to the White House,
accepted an honorary membership
from them, then gave the group an
appreciative speech.[16] He also
packed his administration and armies
with America-hating socialists and
communists, some who were
personal friends of Constitution-
loathing Karl Marx, the founder of
modern communism. An example
was ardent socialist Charles A.
Dana, who was made assistant
secretary of war under Lincoln's
secretary of war, Edwin M.
Stanton.[17] One of the many
communists who served as an officer
in the Union army was General
August von Willich, a Prussian born,
Marxist-schooled radical.[18] After
fighting with the European "Forty-
eighters" in an attempt to destroy
the monarchy,[19] he immigrated to
America in 1853, where he headed a
German-American workers' party.[20]

Reason 10

The "significant victories" gained by the U.S. army under Lincoln's officers were not won fairly, honorably, or humanely as we have been taught in our pro-North history books. Quite the contrary. In fact, more often than not they were the result of scorched-earth, total war policies that included larceny, wide confiscation and destruction of civilian property, rape, maiming, torture, and the mass murder of Southern noncombatants. All were performed, of course, under the approving eye of the U.S. military's commander-in-chief: President Abraham Lincoln.[21]

Reason 11

As a consequence of Lincoln's orders and sanctions, by the end of his war in April 1865 some 500,000 Southern farms and plantations had gone bankrupt, become insolvent, or were ruined; real property value had plummeted 30 percent; and between 10 and 25 percent of the South's inhabitants were dead. Most of Dixie's cities were desolate, the total assessed property evaluation of the Southern states had decreased by 43 percent, and two-thirds of her railroads were gone. In Mississippi alone, one-third of the state's white men were killed or disabled. All of this was a direct result of Lincoln's savagery, greed, vanity, and stupidity.[22]

Reason 12

While Union crimes against the South—such as the illegal harassment, arrest, imprisonment, beating, torture, and even murder of both Southern soldiers and civilian—were being perpetrated, Lincoln spent his time engaging in numerous Victorian frivolities, such as attending theater, balls, and parties, commenting on "pretty ladies" visiting the White House, thanking his followers for sending him presents (such as "Mackinaw salmon trout"), and discussing the intricacies of Shakespeare.[23]

Reason 13

Widely known for his cruelty and swinish behavior, once, while touring the bloody, body-littered battlefield of Sharpsburg (Antietam to Yanks), Lincoln ordered a cheerful minstrel tune to be played, much to the revulsion of his officers and the fury of the local Southern populace.[24]

Reason 14

Lincoln's reputation for cold-blooded callousness was legendary. For instance, when it was reported to him that one of his officers, Edwin H. Stoughton, had been captured by the Confederacy, the president replied: "I don't mind so much the loss of a general—I can make another in five minutes. It's the horses I hate to lose."[25]

Reason 15

Lincoln's contemporaries often commented upon the president's curmudgeonly personality, stating that he "had no heart," that he "seldom praised anybody," and that "he did nothing out of mere gratitude."[26]

Reason 16

Along with Lincoln's sour disposition, he was also reported to be churlish and selfish. One observer affirmed that the president "forgot the devotion of his warmest partisans as soon as the occasion for their services passed." He had not, it was further noted, a single "particle of sympathy with the great mass of his fellow-citizens who were engaged in similar scrambles for place."[27]

Reason 17

Another unlikeable Lincoln trait
that his devotees never mention
is that he was often oblivious of
his surroundings, and could even
be anti-social. During his
inauguration ceremony, for
example, he insisted on kissing
all thirty-four girls (representing
the thirty-four states then in the
Union) in a parade, making both
the young women and onlookers
squirm with discomfort. This
with the country on the verge of
war and in a fearful and deadly
serious mood.[28]

Reason 18

Also known to be superficial, heedless, and inconsiderate, during the War President Lincoln would often entertain himself at public receptions by calling other tall men up to the stage to measure their height against his own.[29] Again, this was at a time when thousands of Americans were dying violent deaths on the battlefield.

Reason 19

Lacking even a shred of social propriety, Lincoln often unthinkingly dressed himself each morning in front of an open White House window, much to the shock and dismay of both his staff and passersby.[30]

Reason 20

Nationally acknowledged as rude, discourteous, and a poor communicator, Lincoln—the president who seemed to prefer the taste of his own foot over anything else—was perpetually apologizing for an inadvertent gaffe; or more often, for an insult he had flung at someone.[31]

Reason 21

Lincoln was described by many as having been crude and unrefined. As proof, observers cited the types of men the president was most likely to spend his time with. These were considered to be the "coarsest men on the list of his acquaintances—low, vulgar, unfortunate creatures," whom, it was said, he heartlessly used as mere "tools."[32]

Reason 22

Many of Lincoln's contemporaries reported that the "moody," "strange," "contradictory," "unsocial," and "gloomy" president was, not surprisingly, unpleasant company. Known for being intensely tightlipped, overly cautious, and unnecessarily inhospitable, it is little wonder that so many people shunned his companionship.[33]

Reason 23

It is well-known that Lincoln suffered from severe depression (then called melancholia), "hypochondriasm," and a host of other psychoneurotic complexes, including a mother fixation, fear of his father, an overdeveloped super-ego, and narcissism. While these are not legitimate reasons to dislike our sixteenth president, as the leader of the globe's most powerful nation, he did seem to be unnecessarily "morbid," as observers referred to him. In the 1830s, for instance, Lincoln wrote a poem called "Suicide,"[34] while in 1842, he began a letter to his friend Joshua F. Speed with these words: "How miserably things seem to be arranged in this world."[35] The joyless president, who seemed to long for death, had countless premonitions and even vivid dreams of his premature demise, all which were fulfilled on April 15, 1865, just weeks after his fifty-sixth birthday.[36]

Reason 24

Lincoln was overtly guileful and untrustworthy. Even his few close associates noted with disdain the president's air of cunning, secretiveness, and craftiness. This made him difficult to deal with and impossible to trust. Of him Lincoln's Secretary of War Edwin M. Stanton commented: "I met Lincoln at the [attorneys'] bar and found him a low, cunning clown." Likewise, Lincoln's friend, business partner, and biographer William H. Herndon wrote: "The first impression of a stranger, on seeing Mr. Lincoln walk, was that he was a tricky man."[37] It is little wonder the duplicitous statesman was given the reverse nickname "Honest Abe."[38]

Reason 25

The ultimate demagogue, Lincoln was often described as a man who presented to the world a host of bizarre and appalling "contrasts and contradictions of character," making him the personification of a political chameleon. As such, he could say what people wanted to hear while conspiring his own villainous schemes behind closed doors. As Lincoln's senatorial opponent Stephen A. Douglas once put it, Lincoln could simultaneously pretend to be a "proslavery man in the south and a negro-equality advocate in the north"—whatever it took to get the majority vote.[39]

Reason 26

Coarse and unsophisticated, Lincoln was widely known for his off-color, even vulgar and inappropriate jokes and bawdy stories, which he loved to tell in front of both his more sophisticated cabinet members and, to the horror of Victorian society, women. This is why Yankee General George B. McClellan called the president "the original gorilla" and "a teller of low stories," while one of Mary Chesnut's friends termed him "the ugliest, most uncouth, the nastiest joker." U.S. President John Tyler's son, famed historian Lyon G. Tyler, made (as did many others) reference to Lincoln's "grotesque humor," "coarse suggestions," and "base insinuations."[40]

Reason 27

Though Lincoln's personal
characteristics, habits, and
behavior were certainly
disturbing and unpresidential, it
was his many war crimes that
make him truly unlikeable. As a
Liberal who, for example,
publicly declared his dislike for
the U.S. Constitution, it is not
surprising to learn that he
repeatedly trampled upon our
nation's most sacred document,
ignoring its clauses, disregarding
it laws, and in general greatly
disrespecting it.[41]

Reason 28

A progressive who clearly abhorred the First Amendment, during his war on the South and states' rights Lincoln found it easy to give himself the unconstitutional power to suppress his opponents in the North by shutting down over 300 hundred pro-peace Yankee newspapers. In most cases he had the owners illegally arrested and imprisoned,[42] after which he confiscated or even destroyed their printing presses.[43]

Reason 29

Besides curbing the press and violating the First Amendment, Lincoln used numerous other nefarious tactics to silence his critics, such as arresting and deporting Northern antiwar advocates. One of the more famous of these was the case of the Conservative Ohio Congressman Clement L. Vallandigham, who, though a civilian, Lincoln had tried in a military court. Denied a writ of *habeas corpus*, the Yankee politician was then deported to the Confederacy. All of these actions are illegal under the Constitution.[44]

Reason 30

It was not just pro-peace politicians that Lincoln went after. He also arbitrarily arrested and tried (by military commission) civilian draft resistors and others suspected of what he self-servingly and incorrectly termed "disloyalty" to the U.S. government.[45]

Reason 31

To further cut off criticism while suppressing communications between his offices and the outside world, during the War Lincoln seized all rail and telegraph lines leading to and from the capital.[46]

Reason 32

Lincoln not only disrupted the telegraph lines in and around Washington, D.C., he went so far as to censor telegraph communications in all areas of the Northern states that he considered to be in sympathy with the "rebellion."[47] As Confederate President Jefferson Davis pointed out, in doing so he went against the Constitution by abandoning the protection of the unalienable rights of the Northern people.[48]

Reason 33

To make sure that both his Northern constituents and his armies took him seriously, Lincoln resorted to torturing both Union soldiers accused of desertion and peaceful unarmed Northern citizens accused of espousing antiwar sentiment (which tyrant Lincoln incorrectly referred to as "treason"). The president's preferred methods of punishment were "violent cold water torture" and being suspended by handcuffed wrists.[49] Worse still, Confederate prisoners were sometimes forced to receive potentially lethal injections of intentionally poisoned "vaccinations" for nonexistent diseases.[50] Meanwhile Confederate supporters, both white and black, were often subjected to horrific torments, such as being hung up by their thumbs for extended periods of time.[51]

Reason 34

While the Southern states participated in the 1860 presidential election, none voted for Lincoln. To prevent a repeat of this embarrassment and to ensure his reelection at all costs, four years later, during the 1864 election, Lincoln illegally prohibited former Confederates, supporters of the Confederacy, and even the eleven states of the Confederacy themselves from voting. (The latter move was both absurd and unnecessary, of course: at the time the Southern states were part of a foreign country, the Confederate States of America, and had no desire or legal right to participate in U.S. elections.)[52]

Reason 35

One of the more sinister ploys Liberal Lincoln used to get reelected in 1864 was to throw out the votes of Democratic (at that time, Conservative) soldiers as "defective." At other times he replaced Democratic ballots with Republican (at the time, Liberal) ones. On numerous occasions he refused to count Democratic (Conservative) votes at all.[53]

Reason 36

There seems to have been no
lengths Lincoln would not go to
guarantee his reelection in 1864.
On June 20, 1863, for example,
he generated five additional
electoral votes for himself by
illegally creating the thirty-fifth
state, West Virginia. (Note: It is
unlawful for a section of a state
to secede from the parent state
without the parent state's
approval—which the Virginia
legislature did not give in this
instance.) As a result, West
Virginia's statehood has never
been officially ratified. [54]

Reason 37

Shortly thereafter, Lincoln insidiously admitted the thirty-sixth state, Nevada, on October 31, a mere week before election day, November 8, 1864. His purpose was, again, to accrue additional electoral votes. The unethical move indeed benefitted him, for as with the 1860 election, he won the 1864 election with less than 50 percent of the popular vote. It was only the Electoral College that allowed our most corrupt chief executive to win a second term.[55]

Reason 38

It was not, however, merely the Electoral College that enabled Lincoln's 1864 victory at the polls. It was said by his contemporaries that Lincoln's use of spies, detectives, "secret agents," fraud, privately hired vigilante gangs, and bribery not only insured his win, but resulted in "the foulest corruptions"—said to have been obvious at every level of his party.[56] The Lincoln administration was truly a thugocracy, headed by an avaricious and immoral tyrant.

Reason 39

During the 1864 election Lincoln stationed armed U.S. soldiers at the polls in order to intimidate voters into casting their ballots for him.[57] To further ensure a win, he insincerely established the holiday we now call "Thanksgiving Day," setting the date on the last Thursday of November. This gave his 2 million soldiers an excuse to "head home for the holidays" in late October and early November, just in time for the November elections. Naturally, grateful Union soldiers went to the polls in huge numbers to vote overwhelmingly for the man who had granted them this holiday respite, an unexpected opportunity to get away from the cold, hunger, filth, dangers, and general horror of the battlefield.[58]

Reason 40

As part of his war on the South and the Constitution Lincoln illegally forced foreigners (i.e., citizens of the Confederate States of America) to take an oath of allegiance to the United States of America, or face arrest and imprisonment.[59] Those who refused not only risked jail time, but often had their homes burned to the ground by vengeful Yankee troops. In fact, thousands of the South's beautiful antebellum houses, and thousands of innocent Southern families were made homeless refugees, by Lincoln and his military henchmen in just this manner.[60]

Reason 41

During his war Lincoln illegally suspended the writ of *habeas corpus* across the entire U.S., and for the first time in our country's history. Though this act was clearly a violation of the Constitution, Lincoln claimed he had an imaginary right he termed "military necessity," required due to the so-called "rebellion" in the South. After the War, in 1886, this legal shenanigan was challenged and overturned by the Supreme Court in the Constitutional landmark case *ex parte Milligan*. According to the Court's justices, the Constitution cannot be suspended in time of emergency—a ruling that it has never rescinded, even up to the present day. Thus, no less than the Supreme Court ruled Lincoln's megalomanic powers unconstitutional.[61]

Reason 42

To assist in the winning of his war Lincoln assumed the extraordinary right of "extraordinary powers." Because there was no such power listed in the Constitution at the time,[62] this was unconstitutional and therefore illegal.[63] It was because of this, as well as the president's other countless crimes, that Yankee socialist-abolitionist Wendell Phillips said: "I judge Mr. Lincoln by his acts, his violations of the law, his overthrow of liberty in the Northern States. I judge Mr. Lincoln by his words and deeds, and so judging him, I am unwilling to trust Abraham Lincoln with the future of this country. Mr. Lincoln is a politician; politicians are like the bones of a horse's fore shoulder—not a straight one in it."[64]

Reason 43

Lincoln stalled issuing the Emancipation Proclamation for as long as possible, only releasing it on January 1, 1863, nearly three years after he had been elected president.[65] Even then he only issued his most famous edict due to pressure from Yankee socialists and communists (deceptively referred to in mainstream history books as "radicals" or "abolitionists")[66] whose votes he needed for his upcoming reelection—and because, by then, he needed more soldiers for his armies. Thus the Final Emancipation Proclamation was nothing more than a sneaky ploy to induce black military recruitment, as a careful reading of the document reveals.[67] Indeed, he often bluntly, blatantly, and correctly referred to it, not as a black civil rights emancipation, but as a "military emancipation."[68]

Reason 44

Lincoln was a zealous anti-abolitionist, which is why he supported the Corwin Amendment (which would have allowed American slavery, in both the North and the South, to continue in perpetuity in exchange for the return of the seceded Southern states),[69] and postponed emancipation for nearly three years into his presidency, prompting socialists and communists ("abolitionists") to angrily call him the "tortoise president"—even though most of them had campaigned for him. As Lincoln himself once said when questioned about whether he was concerned about having a few true abolitionists in the Republican party: "As long as I'm not tarred with the abolitionist brush."[70]

Reason 45

As proof of Lincoln's apathy toward slavery and black civil rights, we have his Inaugural Address, delivered March 4, 1861, in which the anti-abolitionist president clearly stated: "I have no purpose, directly or indirectly, to interfere with the institution of slavery in the States where it exists. I believe I have no lawful right to do so, and I have no inclination to do so." Lincoln was no abolitionist. But he was a sexist, one who refused to lift even a finger to aid in the social advancement of females; this despite the fact that the women's rights movement was raging during the time of his presidency. Subsequently, women did not get the vote until 1920, and true equality did not come until 1972 (with the passage of the Equal Rights Amendment), 107 years after Lincoln's death.[71]

Reason 46

In truth, when it came to slavery Lincoln was what was called a "restrictionist"; that is, one who did not want to completely eradicate it, but merely confine it to where it already existed.[72] Just two years before becoming president, for example, Lincoln said: I would like to keep slavery "at the position in which our [Founding] fathers originally placed it—restricting it from the new [Western] Territories where it had not gone, and legislating to cut off its source by the abrogation of the slave-trade, thus putting the seal of legislation against its spread."[73]

Reason 47

As president, anti-abolitionist Lincoln routinely prohibited the emancipation of slaves by his cabinet members and Union military officers. Among them were such men as General John C. Frémont, General David Hunter, John W. Phelps, Jim Lane, and General Simon Cameron. While we may dislike Lincoln for his anti-abolition activities, they do prove once and for all, if nothing else does, that he did not wage war against the South over slavery.[74] Indeed, on August 15, 1864, the president himself said: "My enemies pretend I am now carrying on this war for the sole purpose of abolition. So long as I am President, it shall be carried on for the sole purpose of restoring the Union."[75]

Reason 48

Abraham Lincoln, one of the world's most outspoken and flagrant white racists, often used the word "nigger," constantly referred to blacks (as he did all non-whites) as an "inferior race," and held that African-Americans should not be allowed to vote, sit on juries, hold political office, or intermarry with whites. "We cannot make them equals," he consistently maintained both privately and publicly.[76]

Reason 49

Lincoln held special contempt for Mexicans, disparagingly referring to them as "mongrels" and "greasers." Naturally, he lumped them in with blacks as just another one of the "inferior races."[77]

Reason 50

Lincoln was a classic white supremacist who believed that European-Americans were racially superior to African-Americans, Native-Americans, Hispanic-Americans, and Asian-Americans.[78] Concerning the first group in this list, for instance, Lincoln made the following comment on July 17, 1858: "Certainly the negro is not our equal in color—perhaps not in many other respects."[79]

Reason 51

Lincoln, who held that the
presence of blacks in America
constituted a racial problem,[80]
often noted that the U.S.
government "was made for the
white people and not for the
negroes."[81]

Reason 52

Lincoln was a rank and file white segregationist and separatist, and a lifelong supporter of the American Colonization Society, a group whose stated mission was to "make America white from coast to coast" by deporting all blacks in the U.S. to foreign countries. The areas where Lincoln wanted to colonize evicted American blacks included Europe, Latin America, and the Caribbean, though he had specific interest in Liberia, Haiti, Belize, and Panama. He actually succeeded in setting up colonies in these four nations, but all four ended in disaster for the African-Americans he exiled there, with death rates of over 50 percent in some cases.[82]

Reason 53

Due to Lincoln's overt racism he has long been held in high esteem by other white racists, all—right into the present day—who have considered him one of their most enduring heroes.[83] Among them have been William P. Pickett (of New York), James K. Vardaman (of Mississippi), and Thomas Dixon Jr. (of North Carolina, whose writings inspired David W. Griffith's famous and much-discussed film on the Ku Klux Klan, *The Birth of a Nation*).[84]

Reason 54

Lincoln did not just support the American Colonization Society as a card carrying member. Shortly before becoming president of the United States he headed the Illinois chapter of the ACS,[85] donated money to the organization,[86] and drew up his own detailed plans for deporting then colonizing American blacks outside the U.S.[87]

Reason 55

When it came to the idea of race, Lincoln's main interest was always American apartheid: the physical segregation of whites and blacks. Why? Because he maintained that blacks threatened to dilute the "racial purity" of European-Americans[88] while taking away jobs and housing from whites.[89] Thus, on July 17, 1858, he declared: "What I would most desire would be the separation of the white and black races."[90] If that proved unworkable, our most racist president noted publicly, he would heartily endorse the idea of putting African-Americans in their own all black state.[91]

Reason 56

Lincoln's favorite person was Kentucky slave owner Henry Clay, whom the president called "my beau ideal."[92] Why? In part because, like Lincoln, Clay was a member of the American Colonization Society. Indeed, at the time of his death in 1852, Clay was the organization's president,[93] which is one of the main reasons Lincoln gave the eulogy at Clay's funeral. It was at this event that fellow ACS leader Lincoln said of black colonization: "May it indeed be realized." Ridding the U.S. of its entire black population would be a "glorious consummation," he went on to assert.[94]

Reason 57

Lincoln's enthusiasm for the idea of "cleansing" the U.S. of its black population can be traced back to his early days as a young politician. In 1858, for example, then a former U.S. representative and Illinois legislator, he made the following public statement regarding the "problem" of African-Americans: "My first impulse would be to free all the slaves, and send them to Liberia [Africa], to their own native land."[95]

Reason 58

One of Lincoln's greatest fears was the intermarriage and subsequent interbreeding of whites and non-whites, or what he termed "amalgamation"—the scientific term which is miscegenation.[96] "There is a natural disgust in the minds of nearly all white people, to the idea of an indiscriminate amalgamation of the white and black races," Lincoln avowed during his famous Dred Scott Speech at Springfield, Illinois.[97] Believing slavery to be the main cause of race-mixing,[98] he pushed to strengthen laws that restricted slavery to areas outside the North.[99] His ultimate solution to this "problem," of course, was black deportation.[100]

Reason 59

Though you would never know it from reading pro-North books on Lincoln, he openly campaigned for black colonization throughout his entire presidency, discussing it, for instance, in great detail in his Second Annual Message to Congress (delivered December 1, 1862). It was here that he made the infamous comment: "I cannot make it better known than it already is, that I strongly favor colonization."[101]

Reason 60

Lincoln pushed for black deportation in both his District of Columbia Emancipation Act (issued April 16, 1862)[102] and in his *Preliminary* Emancipation Proclamation (issued September 22, 1862). Lincoln's colonization clause was only removed from the latter document because his cabinet advised him that he would lose the abolitionist-socialist-communist vote otherwise. Thus, the *Final* Proclamation Emancipation—best known to the public and issued January 1, 1863—was not the one Lincoln wanted. It was the one forced upon him by political expediency.[103]

Reason 61

While Lincoln's defenders eagerly maintain (or pretend) that he gave up on colonization before he became president of the U.S., in reality he continued to promote his plan to deport all blacks out of the U.S. right up until the day he died. Just hours before his assassination, for example, the president met with one of his military men, Union General Benjamin F. Butler, to discuss black colonization. According to Butler's personal memoirs, after the Yankee officer discussed his own ideas for "sending all the blacks away," Lincoln replied encouragingly: "There is meat in that, General Butler; there is meat in that."[104]

Reason 62

Lincoln accused the Confederacy of treason against the United States (an impossibility since the C.S.A. was formed legally under the Constitution's Ninth and Tenth Amendments). Actually, it was Lincoln who committed treason: in the 1840s he put U.S. forces in Mexico at risk by repeatedly issuing antiwar statements about the Mexican-American War (1846-1848). Even more serious, in private he came out against supplying U.S. forces stationed and fighting there. According to Stephen A. Douglas, Lincoln would have gone public and voted against appropriating funds and men to prosecute the war had he been a member of Congress at the time.[105]

Reason 63

After becoming president and launching his war against the South, the Constitution, and states' rights, white supremacist Liberal Lincoln prohibited both blacks and Indians from enlisting in the U.S. military. Blacks (mainly light-skinned) who managed to enlist without being noticed, were soon caught and "honorably discharged."[106] Lincoln only later gave in to non-white recruitment when disease, desertion, defection, and death among his white soldiers required a massive new supply of man power.[107]

Reason 64

Even after officially permitting blacks to enlist with the issuance of his African-American "military measure," better known as the Final Emancipation Proclamation (January 1, 1863), Lincoln would not allow them to fight as armed soldiers.[108] Instead, as that document clearly states, the Union army's newly recruited blacks were to be assigned simple guard duty of "forts, positions, stations, and other places, and to man vessels of all sorts in said service."[109] Few blacks wanted the job, of course, especially after learning of Lincoln's involuntary black recruitment policy: African-Americans who refused to join the Union army were beaten, whipped, and even shot to death where they stood. Those blacks who made it through this barbaric and illegal process alive then had to deal with unequal pay, racist treatment, slave-like duties, and limits on promotion, among numerous other indignities.[110]

Reason 65

While we have been taught that
Lincoln was "the black man's best
friend," nothing could be further
from the truth. Until the day he
died, he did all he could to block
black civil rights, prohibiting
African-Americans from
becoming U.S. citizens, marrying
whites, sitting on juries, voting,
or holding political office.[111]
None of these rights came, in
fact, until *after* Lincoln's death in
April 1865. The so-called "Great
Emancipator" was not even
responsible for "freeing the
slaves," as Northern myth
maintains: since his emancipation
was only active in the
Confederacy (a foreign nation in
which he had no authority), not a
single American slave was
liberated.[112] The truth is that full
official abolition—across the
entire U.S.—did not come until
December 6, 1865, with the
passage of the Thirteenth
Amendment, eight months after
Lincoln's assassination.[113]

Reason 66

One of the many purposes behind Lincoln's Final Emancipation Proclamation was his hope that freed Southern slaves would riot, overthrow the plantations, kill their white owners, and create social, racial, and political chaos across Dixie. This insane plan completely miscarried: not a single slave rebellion occurred in the South at any time during his war; not even after he issued his fake and illegal edict.[114] Nonetheless, Lincoln's diabolic attempt at race warfare, along with his many other racist policies, have left a permanent scar on the American landscape, the ramifications which haunt South and North to this day.

Reason 67

During his war Lincoln unlawfully ordered a naval blockade of Southern ports (unlawful because he never recognized the Confederacy as a separate nation and war had not yet been officially declared).[115] Though his illicit blockade indeed helped him win the conflict, it came at great cost: the U.S. not only earned the world's condemnation for disregarding national maritime law, but the blockade disrupted the South and the North's once mutually beneficial trade, upset world commerce, and caused massive global deprivations (for example, in England).[116]

Reason 68

To stifle resistance toward the U.S. and whip up fear, dissension, and chaos among the Southern people (always a favorite ploy of the Left), Lincoln completely removed every inhabitant living in certain counties, **"en masse,"** as he brusquely put it, in the Southern states. This included thousands of Confederate Jews, who the anti-Semitic president had "expelled" from their homes across large sections of the South—essentially turning all law-abiding Southern Jews into criminals.[117]

Reason 69

War criminal Lincoln "checked"
(i.e., arrested) clergymen who
had "become dangerous to the
public interest"—that is, priests
who contradicted him or who
campaigned for peace with the
South.[118]

Reason 70

Lincoln declared all medicines contraband of war, which helped kill countless thousands of Southerners, both soldiers and civilians—not to mention thousands of Yankee soldiers held in Confederate prisons.[119]

Reason 71

Lincoln threatened war on any nation, particularly England and France, if they in any way supported, aided, or recognized the Confederacy. Though not necessarily illegal, this was highly unethical, for the U.S. herself had long insisted on the right to assist "belligerent" nations, for example, in 1793, 1841, and 1855. Why then did he do it? Had Europe been permitted to give her official recognition and assistance to the South, Lincoln knew he could never win his war against the Confederacy and the Constitution.[120]

Reason 72

Lincoln outrageously and unconstitutionally proclaimed Confederate privateersmen "insurgents" and "pirates," subject to the death penalty. However, privateering, that is, working on an armed privately-owned vessel, was and still is a perfectly legal profession.[121]

Reason 73

Lincoln intimidated judges in an attempt to force them to rule in favor of his war and his liberal, anti-Constitution, big government policies.[122] Not only that, during his four-year stay in the White House he greatly enlarged the U.S. government, adding countless numbers of new positions, departments, and programs to an already oversized and ever growing socialistic behemoth. Among Lincoln's "contributions" to the Federal government were the Department of Agriculture, the National Academy of Science, and the Bureau of Printing and Engraving. He also nationalized the banking system and the railroads, all which the Founding Fathers had worked so hard to prevent. It is little wonder that when President Franklin D. Roosevelt needed a name for his socialistic domestic policies, he borrowed the term that Lincoln used for his own: "New Deal."[123]

Reason 74

Lincoln closed the post office in
an effort to prevent anti-Lincoln,
antiwar mail from being sent or
delivered.[124]

Reason 75

Not only did Lincoln illegally nationalize the railroads,[125] he also forced all Federal employees to contribute 5 percent of their annual income to his 1864 re-election campaign.[126]

Reason 76

Lincoln refused to exchange military prisoners with the Confederacy, which contributed to the unnecessary deaths of thousands of soldiers, both Confederate and Union.[127]

Reason 77

On numerous occasions Lincoln
defied the U.S. Supreme Court,
totally disregarding both its
personal rulings against him and
its constitutional
responsibilities.[128] He also
delayed calling Congress into
session for the first four months
of his first term in order to avoid
facing charges of usurping the
Constitution.[129]

Reason 78

Lincoln instituted the largest number of military drafts in U.S. history, all for a war that he himself created in an effort to install big government at Washington, D.C. One result of Lincoln's compulsory conscription was the New York City Draft Riots of July 1863. During the four-day melee, racist white Northerners targeted not Lincoln, but blacks, who they harassed, beat, and even lynched. At least 500 people, mostly blacks, perished. Afterward, Lincoln refused to conduct an inquiry into the white racist bloodbath, callously commenting: "Better let the dirt alone."[130]

Reason 79

Lincoln illegally fabricated heretofore unknown offices, such as "military governor," in conquered Southern states.[131] In these same states he also illegally imposed so-called "Reconstruction" policies and governments on the populace (the Constitution gives the president no such power).[132]

Reason 80

Lincoln used the U.S. military to prevent Northern state legislatures from meeting,[133] then nullified their legislative acts.[134]

Reason 81

Lincoln invaded Northern states without permission or authority for the purpose of subverting their governments and overthrowing the sovereignty of the people. After illegally shutting down the governments of entire Northern states and declaring martial law without authority,[135] he arrested and imprisoned members of their state legislatures (usually for suspicion of advocating peace with the South). One of the more notable of these was the state of Maryland, which originally had hoped to join the Confederacy. Lincoln's unconstitutional closure of the Old Line State's government, while placing large areas under military rule, prevented any hope Maryland had of uniting with the South.[136]

Reason 82

Lincoln unlawfully established U.S. military rule in a foreign nation (the C.S.A.), and even within states that were still part of the Union (such as Missouri).[137]

Reason 83

Lincoln inaugurated America's first federal monetary monopoly.[138]

Reason 84

Conservative estimates hold that Lincoln imprisoned between 38,000 and 50,000 *Northern* civilians (men, women, and children), without trial, many for as long as four years (the duration of the entire war).[139]

Reason 85

Lincoln illegally incarcerated civilians, like Confederate Vice President Alexander H. Stephens, in military prisons.[140]

Reason 86

Liberal Lincoln levied the first personal income tax, launching what would later become the Internal Revenue Service (IRS).[141]

Reason 87

In an attempt to suppress pro-South sentiment in the North, Lincoln trampled on the Constitution by prohibiting governmental debate over secession.[142]

Reason 88

Lincoln ordered the first and only mass execution (and that of his own citizens) by a president in U.S. history.[143]

Reason 89

Big government Lincoln, who, as we have seen, surrounded himself with socialists, communists, and Marxists (including the notorious radical European Leftists known as the Forty-eighters),[144] purposefully and guilefully changed the *meaning* of the term the U.S. from plural (i.e., the "United States") to singular (i.e., a "United State"). The Founding Fathers, of course, intended the former meaning.[145]

Reason 90

Lincoln established martial law and provisional courts in conquered Confederate states (illegal because the South's own civilian courts remained open during the War).[146] After using state conventions to assume unlawful powers, he forced the election and introduction of his own hand-picked individuals to offices still occupied.[147]

Reason 91

Hypocrite Lincoln encouraged the western area of Virginia to secede (illegally creating the state of West Virginia) while he was at war with the South because she had seceded.[148]

Reason 92

White racists, white supremacists, racial separatists, and big government Liberals are not the only ones who adore Lincoln. Because he overthrew the confederate government of delegated and limited powers created by the Southern Founding Fathers and replaced it with an oversized, overly powerful, centralized, military despotism, Lincoln has become the darling of dictators, totalitarians, tyrants, autocrats, and despots around the world. Among them was German dictator Adolf Hitler, head of the National Socialist German Workers Party (the Nazis), who was fond of citing Lincoln as a shining example of how to destroy states' rights.[149] Another admirer was communist extremist Karl Marx, who once wrote the U.S. president a glowing letter of appreciation, encouraging him in his "reconstruction of a social world."[150]

Reason 93

A spiteful and petulant Lincoln signed an order for the arrest of the U.S. Supreme Court's Chief Justice Roger B. Taney, simply because Taney had correctly told him that suspending *habeas corpus* was unconstitutional and therefore illegal.[151]

Reason 94

Liberal Lincoln—an economic protectionist, mercantilist, and interventionist, who supported the ideas of corporate welfare (then called "internal improvements") and a nationalized banking system—put a stop to the tremendous economic growth of the 1850s, forced the nation into a hyperinflationary state, and terminated the vital connection between the currency and precious metals.[152] While all of this was going on he issued paper money (imaginary tender, or what Thomas Jefferson called "fictitious capital"), at a time when the U.S. economy could least afford to go into debt.[153]

Reason 95

Anti-Semitic Lincoln prohibited Jews from serving as military chaplains. By his order, only ordained Christian ministers were allowed to fill the positions.[154] This despite the fact that a Jew, the politically Conservative Judah Benjamin, served variously as the Confederacy's state attorney, secretary of war, and secretary of state.[155]

Reason 96

In order to prevent international support of the Confederacy, during his war Lincoln and his hired gangs of thugs subjected foreign visitors to the U.S. to new passport regulations.[156] He also illegally forced citizens of the Confederate States of America (who were also foreigners) to take an oath of allegiance to the United States of America, or face arrest and imprisonment.[157]

Reason 97

Lincoln claimed that he had the authority to, as he put it, "suppress insurrection." However, according to the U.S. Constitution, Article 1, Section 8, Clause 15, only Congress has this power.[158]

Reason 98

Lincoln never once acknowledged the Confederate States of America as a separate, legitimate, and constitutionally formed country, nor did he ever formally recognize Jefferson Davis as the C.S.A.'s president.[159] Yet he nonsensically and disingenuously claimed that he had originally invaded the South "for the sole purpose of restoring the Union."[160]

Reason 99

Prior to 1860 Lincoln firmly believed that he was not worthy of becoming president of the United States. "Just think of such a sucker as me as President," he once commented. "I must in candor say I do not think myself fit for the Presidency," he said further.[161] Despite these odd misgivings, the man who won both the 1860 and the 1864 elections with less than 50 percent of the popular American vote,[162] and who only two years earlier had been pronounced unqualified to be a U.S. senator by the American people, became our sixteenth president.[163] Not surprisingly, the dictatorial left-wing demagogue was voted the worst chief executive in American history up until that time.[164]

The End

NOTES

1. For more on the nihilistic, atheistic, anti-life, anti-tradition, anti-American, anti-Constitution, anti-capitalism, anti-South agenda of the Victorian Republican Party (then the Liberal Party) and the modern Democrat Party (now the Liberal Party), otherwise known as "The Communist/Socialist Rules for Revolution," see Hasselberg, pp. 2350-2351; Lenin, passim; Marx and Engels, passim.

2. *Confederate Veteran*, July 1901, Vol. 9, No. 7, p. 318.

3. Seabrook, L (2010 paperback edition unless otherwise indicated), pp. 563-564.

4. Seabrook, L, p. 758.

5. Seabrook, L, pp. 918-938.

6. Amos, p. 354.

7. Seabrook, L, p. 860.

8. Seabrook, L, pp. 863-866.

9. Seabrook, L, p. 130. Also see my book *All We Ask is to be Let Alone: The Southern Secession Fact Book*.

10. Seabrook, ALSV, pp. 111, 120-121.

11. Seabrook, L, pp. 247-311.

12. Seabrook, L, pp. 195-198. For the complete text of the U.S. Constitution, see my book *America's Three Constitutions*.

13. Seabrook, ALSV, p. 303.

14. Seabrook, ALSV, pp. 299-300, 431-432; L, pp. 159-160, 163-164.

15. Seabrook, ALSV, pp. 437-439.

16. Seabrook, ALWALJDWAC, p. 104.

17. Seabrook, ALWALJDWAC, pp. 95, 105-106.

18. Seabrook, ALWALJDWAC, p. 95.

19. Seabrook, HJDA, p. 68; Seabrook, LW, pp. 73-74, 78, 112; Seabrook, ALWALJDWAC, pp. 20, 52, 72-73, 93, 95-96, 100-101, 140, 151.

20. Warner, GB, s.v. "August (von) Willich."

21. Seabrook, ALSV, pp. 304, 415-434.

22. Seabrook, L, p. 847.

23. Seabrook, L, pp. 838-839.

24. Seabrook, ALSV, pp. 470-471.

25. Seabrook, ALSV, p. 471.

26. Seabrook, ALSV, p. 471.

27. Seabrook, ALSV, p. 471.

28. Seabrook, ALSV, p. 472.

29. Seabrook, ALSV, pp. 471-472.

30. Seabrook, ALSV, p. 472.

31. Seabrook, ALSV, p. 472.

32. Seabrook, ALSV, p. 472.

33. Seabrook, ALSV, p. 472.

34. Seabrook, ALSV, p. 472.

35. Nicolay and Hay, ALCW, Vol. 1, p. 64.

36. Seabrook, ALSV, pp. 543-545.

37. Seabrook, ALSV, p. 472.

38. Seabrook, HJDA, p. 157.

39. Seabrook, ALSV, pp. 472-473.

40. Seabrook, ALSV, pp. 473, 474.

41. Seabrook, L, pp. 154-201.

42. Seabrook, L, p. 759.

43. Seabrook, ALSV, p. 283.

44. Seabrook, L, pp. 714, 759.

45. Seabrook, L, p. 759.

46. Seabrook, L, p. 759.

47. Seabrook, L, p. 759.

48. Seabrook, ALSV, p. 305.

49. Seabrook, L, p. 759.

50. Seabrook, TBB, pp. 102-103.

51. Seabrook, TBB, p. 316.

52. Seabrook, L, pp. 759, 876-877.

53. Seabrook, L, p. 876.

54. Seabrook, L, pp. 877-880.

55. Seabrook, L, pp. 880-881.

56. Seabrook, L, pp. 719, 759.

57. Seabrook, ALSV, pp. 292-293.

58. Seabrook, L, pp. 870-876.

59. Seabrook, L, pp. 759-760.

60. See e.g., Seabrook, TMCP, pp. 484-487.

61. Seabrook, L, p. 166-171, 760.

62. Seabrook, L, p. 764.

63. Seabrook, L, p. 760.

64. Christian, p. 12.

65. Seabrook, L, pp. 327-328.

66. Seabrook, TBB, pp. 20-24.

67. Seabrook, L, p. 823. See also pp. 654-657.

68. Seabrook, TUAL, pp. 110-111.

69. Seabrook, L (2016 hardcover edition), pp. 373-374; 479.

70. Seabrook, L, p. 312.

71. Seabrook, L, p. 402; ALSV, pp. 315-317.

72. Seabrook, L, pp. 403-409.

73. Seabrook, L, p. 404.

74. Seabrook, L, p. 760.

75. Seabrook, L, p. 905.

76. Seabrook, L, p. 579.

77. Seabrook, L, pp. 581-582.

78. The belief that one race is superior to another is the original and only correct definition of racism—despite claims by the Left to the contrary. Sadly, many dictionary publishers today are altering the definition of racism to fit the sociopolitical agendas of race-baiters, race-merchants, racial divisionists, socialists, communists, and supporters of the intentionally fabricated ideology, "victim culture."

79. Seabrook, L, p. 566.

80. Seabrook, L, p. 577.

81. Seabrook, L, pp. 565, 917.

82. Seabrook, L, pp. 563-633.

83. Seabrook, ALSV, p. 270.

84. Davis, pp. 146-151.

85. Seabrook, ALSV, p. 461.

86. Davis, p. 147.

87. Seabrook, L, p. 608.

88. Seabrook, L, pp. 593-594.

89. Seabrook, L, pp. 419-422, 598-599.

90. Seabrook, TUAL, p. 91.

91. Seabrook, TUAL, p. 81.

92. Seabrook, L, p. 337.

93. Seabrook, ALSV, p. 461.

94. Seabrook, L, p. 597.

95. Seabrook, L, p. 607.

96. Seabrook, L, p. 594.

97. Seabrook, L, pp. 472-473, 575.

98. Seabrook, L, pp. 575-578.

99. Seabrook, L, pp. 404-407.

100. Seabrook, L, pp. 584-633.
101. Seabrook, ALSV, p. 461.
102. Seabrook, L, pp. 80-81, 599-601.
103. Seabrook, L, pp. 614-618.
104. Seabrook, L, pp. 632-633.
105. Seabrook, L, pp. 303-305.
106. Seabrook, ALSV, pp. 119-120.
107. Seabrook, L, p. 655.
108. Seabrook, ALSV, pp. 127-128.
109. Seabrook, L, p. 657.
110. Seabrook, L, pp. 883-917.
111. Seabrook, L, pp. 563, 575, 896-901, 933.
112. Seabrook, L, pp. 649-651.
113. Seabrook, L, pp. 613-614.
114. Seabrook, ALSV, pp. 129-133.
115. Seabrook, L, pp. 190-195, 760.
116. Seabrook, ALSV, p. 304; L, pp. 191-198.
117. Seabrook, L, pp. 760, 933-935.
118. Seabrook, L, p. 760.
119. Seabrook, L, pp. 760-761.
120. Seabrook, L, p. 761.
121. Seabrook, L, p. 761.
122. Seabrook, L, p. 761.
123. Seabrook, ALSV, pp. 491-492.
124. Seabrook, L, p. 761.
125. Seabrook, ALSV, p. 303.
126. Seabrook, L, p. 761.
127. Seabrook, L, p. 761.
128. Seabrook, L, p. 761.
129. Seabrook, ALSV, p. 303.
130. Seabrook, L, pp. 762, 768-770.
131. Seabrook, L, p. 762.
132. Seabrook, ALSV, p. 303.
133. Seabrook, L, p. 762.
134. Seabrook, ALSV, p. 305.
135. Seabrook, ALSV, p. 305.
136. Seabrook, L, p. 762.
137. Seabrook, L, p. 762.
138. Seabrook, L, p. 762.
139. Seabrook, L, p. 762.
140. Seabrook, L, p. 762.
141. Seabrook, L, p. 762.
142. Seabrook, L, p. 762.
143. Seabrook, L, p. 762.
144. Seabrook, HJDA, p. 68; Seabrook, LW, pp. 73-74, 78, 112; Seabrook, ALWALJDWAC, pp. 20, 52, 72-73, 93, 95-96, 100-101, 140, 151.
145. Seabrook, L, pp. 762-763.
146. Seabrook, L, p. 763; ALSV, p. 304.
147. Seabrook, ALSV, p. 305.
148. Seabrook, L, p. 763.
149. Seabrook, L, p. 39.
150. Seabrook, L, pp. 113-114. For the full letter from Marx to Lincoln, see my book ALSV, p. 575.
151. Seabrook, L, p. 763.
152. Seabrook, L, pp. 114, 763.

153. Seabrook, ALSV, p. 303.

154. Seabrook, L, pp. 763-764.

155. Seabrook, HSC, passim.

156. Seabrook, L, p. 764.

157. Seabrook, ALSV, p. 303.

158. Seabrook, L, pp. 764-765.

159. Seabrook, L, pp. 760, 863, 876.

160. Seabrook, L, p. 905.

161. Seabrook, ALSV, p. 545.

162. Seabrook, L, p. 245.

163. Seabrook, L, p. 116.

164. Seabrook, ALSV, p. 486.

BIBLIOGRAPHY

And Suggested Reading

Alotta, Robert I. *Civil War Justice: Union Army Executions Under Lincoln.* Shippensburg, PA: White Mane, 1989.

Amos, J. O. (pub). *Coin World Almanac: A Handbook for Coin Collectors.* Sidney, OH: Amos Press, 1975.

Bennett, Lerone. *Forced into Glory: Abraham Lincoln's White Dream.* Chicago, IL: Johnson Publishing Co., 2000.

Carnahan, Burrus M. *Lincoln on Trial: Southern Civilians and the Law of War.* Lexington, KY: University Press of Kentucky, 2010.

Christian, George L. *Abraham Lincoln: An Address Delivered Before R. E. Lee Camp, No. 1 Confederate Veterans at Richmond, VA, October 29, 1909.* Richmond, VA: L. H. Jenkins, 1909.

Davis, Michael. *The Image of Lincoln in the South.* Knoxville, TN: University of Tennessee Press, 1971.

Emison, John Avery. *Lincoln Über Alles: Dictatorship Comes to America.* Gretna, LA: Pelican Publishing Co., 2009.

Garrison, Webb B. *The Lincoln No One Knows: The Mysterious Man Who Ran the Civil War.* Nashville, TN: Rutledge Hill Press, 1993.

Hasselberg, P. D. (ed.). *Parliamentary Debates: First Session, Fortieth Parliament, 1982, House of Representatives* (Vol. 445). Wellington, New Zealand: Government Printer, 1982.

Lenin, Vladimir. *"Left Wing" Communism: An Infantile Disorder.* Detroit, MI: The Marxian Educational Society, 1921.

Lewis, Lloyd. *Myths After Lincoln.* 1929. New York, NY: The Press of the Reader's Club, 1941 ed.

Maihafer, Harry J. *War of Words: Abraham Lincoln and the Civil War Press.* Dulles, VA: Brassey's, 2001.

Manning, Timothy D., Sr. (ed.) *Lincoln Reconsidered: Conference Reader.* High Point, NC: Heritage Foundation Press, 2006.

Marx, Karl, and Frederick Engels. *Manifesto of the Communist Party.* Chicago, IL: Charles H. Kerr and Co., 1906.

Meriweather, Elizabeth Avery. *Facts and Falsehoods Concerning the War on the South, 1861-1865.* Memphis, TN: A. R. Taylor, 1904.

Minor, Charles Landon Carter. *The Real Lincoln: From the Testimony of His Contemporaries.* Richmond, VA: Everett Waddey Co., 1904.

Mitgang, Herbert (ed.). *Lincoln As They Saw Him.* 1956. New York, NY: Collier, 1962 ed.

Neely, Mark E., Jr. *The Fate of Liberty: Abraham Lincoln and Civil Liberties.* New York, NY: Oxford University Press, 1991.

Nicolay, John G., and John Hay (eds.). *Abraham Lincoln: A History.* 10 vols. New York, NY: The Century Co., 1890.

——. *Complete Works of Abraham Lincoln.* 12 vols. 1894. New York, NY: Francis D. Tandy Co., 1905 ed.

Oates, Stephen B. *Abraham Lincoln: The Man Behind the Myths.* New York, NY: Meridian, 1984.

Pickett, William Passmore. *The Negro Problem: Abraham Lincoln's Solution.* New York, NY: G. P. Putnam's Sons, 1909.

Quarles, Benjamin. *The Negro in the Civil War.* 1953. Cambridge, MA: Da Capo Press, 1988 ed.

——. *Lincoln and the Negro.* 1962. Cambridge, MA: Da Capo Press, 1990 ed.

Randall, James Garfield. *Lincoln: The Liberal Statesman.* New York, NY: Dodd, Mead and Co., 1947.

Remsburg, John B. *Abraham Lincoln: Was He a Christian?* New York, NY: The Truth Seeker Co., 1893.

Rutherford, Mildred Lewis. *A True Estimate of Abraham Lincoln and Vindication of the South.* N.p., n.d.

Seabrook, Lochlainn. *Carnton Plantation Ghost Stories: True Tales of the Unexplained from Tennessee's Most Haunted Civil War House!* 2005. Franklin, TN, 2016 ed.

——. *Nathan Bedford Forrest: Southern Hero, American Patriot.* 2007. Franklin, TN, 2010 ed.

——. *Abraham Lincoln: The Southern View.* 2007. Franklin, TN: Sea Raven Press, 2013 ed.

——. *The McGavocks of Carnton Plantation: A Southern History - Celebrating One of Dixie's Most Noble Confederate Families and Their Tennessee Home.* 2008. Franklin, TN, 2011 ed.

——. *A Rebel Born: A Defense of Nathan Bedford Forrest.* 2010. Franklin, TN: Sea Raven Press, 2011 ed.

——. *Everything You Were Taught About the Civil War is Wrong, Ask a Southerner!* 2010. Franklin, TN: Sea Raven Press, revised 2019 ed.

——. *The Quotable Jefferson Davis: Selections From the Writings and Speeches of the Confederacy's First President.* Franklin, TN: Sea Raven Press, 2011.

——. *The Quotable Robert E. Lee: Selections From the Writings and Speeches of the South's Most Beloved Civil War General.* Franklin, TN: Sea Raven Press, 2011 Sesquicentennial Civil War Edition.

——. *Lincolnology: The Real Abraham Lincoln Revealed In His Own Words.* Franklin, TN: Sea Raven Press, 2011.

——. *The Unquotable Abraham Lincoln: The President's Quotes They Don't Want You To Know!* Franklin, TN: Sea Raven Press, 2011.

——. *Honest Jeff and Dishonest Abe: A Southern Children's Guide to the Civil War.* Franklin, TN: Sea Raven Press, 2012.

——. *Encyclopedia of the Battle of Franklin - A Comprehensive Guide to the Conflict that Changed the Civil War.* Franklin, TN: Sea Raven Press, 2012.

——. *The Quotable Nathan Bedford Forrest: Selections From the Writings and Speeches of the Confederacy's Most Brilliant Cavalryman.* Spring Hill, TN: Sea Raven Press, 2012.

——. *Forrest! 99 Reasons to Love Nathan Bedford Forrest.* Spring Hill, TN: Sea Raven Press, 2012.

——. *Give 'Em Hell Boys! The Complete Military Correspondence of Nathan Bedford Forrest.* Spring Hill, TN: Sea Raven Press, 2012.

——. *The Constitution of the Confederate States of America Explained: A Clause-by-Clause Study of the South's Magna Carta.* Spring Hill, TN: Sea Raven Press, 2012 Sesquicentennial Civil War Edition.

——. *The Great Impersonator: 99 Reasons to Dislike Abraham Lincoln.* Spring Hill, TN: Sea Raven Press, 2012.

——. *The Old Rebel: Robert E. Lee As He Was Seen By His Contemporaries.* Spring Hill, TN: Sea Raven Press, 2012 Sesquicentennial Civil War Edition.

——. *The Quotable Stonewall Jackson: Selections From the Writings and Speeches of the South's Most Famous General.* Spring Hill, TN: Sea Raven Press, 2012 Sesquicentennial Civil War Edition.

——. *Saddle, Sword, and Gun: A Biography of Nathan Bedford Forrest for Teens.* Spring Hill, TN: Sea Raven Press, 2013.

——. *The Alexander H. Stephens Reader: Excerpts From the Works of a Confederate Founding Father*. Spring Hill, TN: Sea Raven Press, 2013.

——. *The Quotable Alexander H. Stephens: Selections From the Writings and Speeches of the Confederacy's First Vice President*. Spring Hill, TN: Sea Raven Press, 2013 Sesquicentennial Civil War Edition.

——. *Give This Book to a Yankee! A Southern Guide to the Civil War for Northerners*. Spring Hill, TN: Sea Raven Press, 2014.

——. *The Articles of Confederation Explained: A Clause-by-Clause Study of America's First Constitution*. Spring Hill, TN: Sea Raven Press, 2014.

——. *Confederate Blood and Treasure: An Interview With Lochlainn Seabrook*. Spring Hill, TN: Sea Raven Press, 2015.

——. *Nathan Bedford Forrest and the Battle of Fort Pillow: Yankee Myth, Confederate Fact*. Spring Hill, TN: Sea Raven Press, 2015.

——. *Everything You Were Taught About American Slavery War is Wrong, Ask a Southerner!* Spring Hill, TN: Sea Raven Press, 2015.

——. *Confederacy 101: Amazing Facts You Never Knew About America's Oldest Political Tradition*. Spring Hill, TN: Sea Raven Press, 2015.

——. *The Great Yankee Coverup: What the North Doesn't Want You to Know About Lincoln's War!* Spring Hill, TN: Sea Raven Press, 2015.

——. *Slavery 101: Amazing Facts You Never Knew About America's "Peculiar Institution."* Spring Hill, TN: Sea Raven Press, 2015.

——. *Confederate Flag Facts: What Every American Should Know About Dixie's Southern Cross*. Spring Hill, TN: Sea Raven Press, 2016.

——. *Nathan Bedford Forrest and the Ku Klux Klan: Yankee Myth, Confederate Fact*. Spring Hill, TN: Sea Raven Press, 2016.

——. *Seabrook's Bible Dictionary of Traditional and Mystical Christian Doctrines*. Spring Hill, TN: Sea Raven Press, 2016.

——. *Everything You Were Taught About African-Americans and the Civil War is Wrong, Ask a Southerner!* Spring Hill, TN: Sea Raven Press, 2016.

——. *Nathan Bedford Forrest and African-Americans: Yankee Myth, Confederate Fact*. Spring Hill, TN: Sea Raven Press, 2016.

——. *Women in Gray: A Tribute to the Ladies Who Supported the Southern Confederacy*. Spring Hill, TN: Sea Raven Press, 2016.

——. *Lincoln's War: The Real Cause, the Real Winner, the Real Loser*. Spring Hill, TN: Sea Raven Press, 2016.

——. *The Unholy Crusade: Lincoln's Legacy of Destruction in the American South*. Spring Hill, TN: Sea Raven Press, 2017.

——. *Abraham Lincoln Was a Liberal, Jefferson Davis Was a Conservative: The Missing Key to Understanding the American Civil War*. Spring Hill, TN: Sea Raven Press, 2017.

——. *All We Ask is to be Let Alone: The Southern Secession Fact Book*. Spring Hill, TN: Sea Raven Press, 2017.

——. *The Ultimate Civil War Quiz Book: How Much Do You Really Know About America's Most Misunderstood Conflict?* Spring Hill, TN: Sea Raven Press, 2017.

——. *Rise Up and Call Them Blessed: Victorian Tributes to the Confederate Soldier, 1861-1901*. Spring Hill, TN: Sea Raven Press, 2017.

——. *Victorian Confederate Poetry: The Southern Cause in Verse, 1861-1901*. Spring Hill, TN: Sea Raven Press, 2018.

——. *Confederate Monuments: Why Every American Should Honor Confederate Soldiers and Their Memorials*. Spring Hill, TN: Sea Raven Press, 2018.

——. *The God of War: Nathan Bedford Forrest as He Was Seen by His Contemporaries*. Spring Hill, TN: Sea Raven Press, 2018.

——. *The Battle of Spring Hill: Recollections of Confederate and Union Soldiers*. Spring Hill, TN: Sea Raven Press, 2018.

——. *I Rode With Forrest! Confederate Soldiers Who Served With the World's Greatest Cavalry Leader*. Spring Hill, TN: Sea Raven Press, 2018.

——. *The Battle of Nashville: Recollections of Confederate and Union Soldiers*. Spring Hill, TN: Sea Raven Press, 2018.

——. *The Battle of Franklin: Recollections of Confederate and Union Soldiers*. Spring Hill, TN: Sea Raven Press, 2018.

——. *A Rebel Born: The Screenplay* (for the film). Written 2011. Franklin, TN: Sea Raven Press, 2020.

——. (ed.) *A Short History of the Confederate States of America* (Jefferson Davis, Belford Company, NY, 1890). A Sea Raven Press Reprint. Spring Hill, TN: Sea Raven Press, 2020.

——. (ed.) *Prison Life of Jefferson Davis: Embracing Details and Incidents in his Captivity, With Conversations on Topics of Public Interest* (John J. Craven, Sampson, Low, Son, and Marston, London, UK, 1866). A Sea Raven Press Reprint. Spring Hill, TN: Sea Raven Press, 2020.

——. *What the Confederate Flag Means to Me: Americans Speak Out in Defense of Southern Honor, Heritage, and History*. Spring Hill, TN: Sea Raven Press, 2021.

——. *Heroes of the Southern Confederacy: The Illustrated Book of Confederate Officials, Soldiers, and Civilians*. Spring Hill, TN: Sea Raven Press, 2021.

——. *Support Your Local Confederate: Wit and Humor in the Southern Confederacy*. Spring Hill, TN: Sea Raven Press, 2021.

——. *America's Three Constitutions: Complete Texts of the Articles of Confederation, Constitution of the United States of America, and Constitution of the Confederate States of America*. Spring Hill, TN: Sea Raven Press, 2021.

——. *Vintage Southern Cookbook: 2,000 Delicious Dishes From Dixie*. Spring Hill, TN: Sea Raven Press, 2021.

——. *The Bittersweet Bond: Race Relations in the Old South as Described by White and Black Southerners*. Spring Hill, TN: Sea Raven Press, 2022.

Tagg, Larry. *The Unpopular Mr. Lincoln: The Story of America's Most Reviled President*. New York, NY: Savas Beatie, 2009.

Tarbell, Ida Minerva. *The Life of Abraham Lincoln*. 4 vols. New York, NY: Lincoln History Society, 1895-1900.

Tilley, John Shipley. *Lincoln Takes Command*. 1941. Nashville, TN: Bill Coats Limited, 1991 ed.

Wilbur, Henry Watson. *President Lincoln's Attitude Towards Slavery and Emancipation: With a Review of Events Before and Since the Civil War*. Philadelphia, PA: W. H. Jenkins, 1914.

MEET THE AUTHOR

NEO-VICTORIAN SCHOLAR LOCHLAINN SEABROOK, a descendant of the families of Alexander Hamilton Stephens, John Singleton Mosby, Edmund Winchester Rucker, and William Giles Harding, is a 7th generation Kentuckian and the most prolific pro-South writer in the world today. Known by literary critics as the "new Shelby Foote" and by his fans as the "Voice of the Traditional South," he is a recipient of the United Daughters of the Confederacy's prestigious Jefferson Davis Historical Gold Medal. As a lifelong writer he has authored and edited books ranging in topics from history, politics, science, and biography, to nature, religion, music, alternative health, and the paranormal, books that his readers describe as "game changers," "transformative," and "life altering."

One of the world's most popular living historians, he is a 17th generation Southerner of Appalachian heritage who descends from dozens of patriotic Revolutionary War soldiers and Confederate soldiers from Kentucky, Tennessee, North Carolina, and Virginia. A proud member of the Sons of the Confederate Veterans, he is a true Renaissance Man. Besides being an accomplished and well respected author-historian and Bible authority, he is also a Kentucky Colonel, eagle scout, screenwriter, nature, wildlife, and landscape photographer, artist, graphic designer, songwriter (3,000 songs), film composer, multi-instrument musician, vocalist, session player, music producer, genealogist, former history museum docent, and a former ranch hand, zookeeper, and wrangler.

Currently Seabrook is the author and editor of nearly 100 adult and children's books (containing a total of some 25,3500 pages and 12,700,900 words) that have earned him accolades from around the globe. His works, which have sold on every continent except Antarctica, have introduced hundreds of thousands to vital facts that have been left out of our mainstream books. He has been endorsed internationally by leading experts, museum curators, award-winning historians, bestselling authors, celebrities, filmmakers, noted scientists, well regarded educators, TV show hosts and producers, renowned military artists, illustrious religious leaders, esteemed heritage organizations, and distinguished academicians of all races, creeds, and colors. Colonel Seabrook holds the world record for writing the most books on Southern icon Nathan Bedford Forrest: 12.

Of northern and central European descent, he is the 6th great-grandson of the Earl of Oxford and a descendant of European royalty. His modern day cousins include: Johnny Cash, Elvis Presley, Lisa Marie Presley, Billy Ray and Miley Cyrus, Patty Loveless, Tim McGraw, Lee Ann Womack, Dolly Parton, Pat Boone, Naomi, Wynonna, and Ashley Judd, Ricky Skaggs, the Sunshin e Sisters, Martha Carson, Chet Atkins, Patrick J. Buchanan, Cindy Crawford, Arthur Conan Doyle, Bertram Thomas Combs (Kentucky's 50th governor), Edith Bolling (second wife of Pres. Woodrow Wilson), Andy Griffith, Riley Keough, George C. Scott, Robert Duvall, Reese Witherspoon, Lee Marvin, Rebecca Gayheart, and Tom Cruise.

A constitutionalist, avid outdoorsman, and gun rights advocate, Colonel Seabrook is the author of the international blockbuster, *Everything You Were Taught About the Civil War is Wrong, Ask a Southerner!* He lives with his wife and family in beautiful historic Middle Tennessee, the heart of the Confederacy.

For more information on author Col. Seabrook visit

LOCHLAINNSEABROOK.COM

If you enjoyed this book you will be interested in Colonel Seabrook's other popular related titles:

☞ ABRAHAM LINCOLN WAS A LIBERAL, JEFFERSON DAVIS WAS A CONSERVATIVE
☞ EVERYTHING YOU WERE TAUGHT ABOUT THE CIVIL WAR IS WRONG, ASK A SOUTHERNER!
☞ ALL WE ASK IS TO BE LET ALONE: THE SOUTHERN SECESSION FACT BOOK
☞ EVERYTHING YOU WERE TAUGHT ABOUT AMERICAN SLAVERY IS WRONG, ASK A SOUTHERNER!
☞ CONFEDERATE FLAG FACTS: WHAT EVERY AMERICAN SHOULD KNOW ABOUT DIXIE'S SOUTHERN CROSS
☞ LINCOLN'S WAR: THE REAL CAUSE, THE REAL WINNER, THE REAL LOSER

Available from Sea Raven Press and wherever fine books are sold

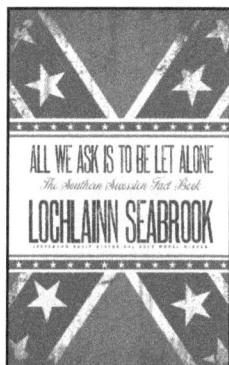

ALL OF OUR BOOK COVERS ARE AVAILABLE AS 11" X 17" POSTERS, SUITABLE FOR FRAMING

SeaRavenPress.com

www.ingramcontent.com/pod-product-compliance
Lightning Source LLC
LaVergne TN
LVHW041228080426
835508LV00011B/1112